Fresh coffee –

the best welcome in the world ...

ETIQUETTE
FOR
COFFEE
LOVERS

Copper Beech Publishing

First published in Great Britain by
Copper Beech Publishing Ltd
© Beryl Peters 1996

ISBN 1 898617 13 9

A CIP catalogue record for this book is available from
the British Library.

Editor: Jan Barnes

Copper Beech Publishing Ltd
P O Box 159 East Grinstead
Sussex England RH19 4FS

'The powers of a man's mind
are directly proportioned to
the quantity of coffee he drinks.'

Sir James Mackintosh
1765 – 1832

INTRODUCTION

Today's coffee lovers might be surprised to know how many times their favourite drink has been in jeopardy over the centuries, having to compete with such well-loved national favourites as cocoa, tea and ale.

In Victorian England, the Temperance Movement encouraged the popularity of coffee as a drink for working people in preference to alcohol.

The history of coffee can be seen through over 1000 years of progress, hindered or helped by pilgrims, popes, kings, pirates, smugglers and business tycoons.

The development of the drink and its rapid spread in the days of difficult travel was in spite of those people who first discovered it and tried to keep coffee a secret!

In the home, servants had to learn how to make coffee and to learn the correct etiquette attached to serving.

Try some of the coffee recipes, and have a go at 'reading the grounds' following in the footsteps of the Cup-Women of a by-gone era.

The very smell of fresh coffee can make the mouth water as it summons up the warmth of the early morning's first drink, the mid-morning break, the busy lunch-time and the after-dinner luxury.

Why not spoil yourself? Make a cup of coffee and as you sip, let your mind take a flight of fancy, recalling some of the famous names such as Bach, Beethoven, Napoleon and others, who were passionate in their love of coffee. From this well-loved drink may have sprung the inspiration for poetical masterpieces, military manoeuvres and great symphonies!

Beryl Peters

COFFEE LEGENDS AND SECRETS

The legends surrounding this drink show what an important and valuable commodity coffee has been over the centuries. Even the origin of its name is in doubt. Some say that the word *coffee* comes from:

KAWECH
an Arabic word meaning strength and vigour
KAHWEH
from the Turks, which means 'exciting'
KAFFA
a province of Ethiopia.

The legend of starvation in the wilderness ...

It is said that an exiled Arabian Sheik saved himself from starvation whilst in the wilderness by making soup from the berries of the coffee plant.

The legend of the goat herder ...

Another tale tells us that Kaldi, a goat herder, observing the frolicsome behaviour of his goats after they had eaten the fruit of the coffee tree, prepared some for himself in the form of a beverage. He and his dervishes so appreciated this new drink that they were in the habit of taking it at night in order to keep them wakeful in their vigils. The goat herder introduced it to the monks in the nearby monastery and it worked on them too, keeping them awake during their long hours of prayer!

𝒯rying to keep the secret ...

As early as the 12th century the Arab countries were cultivating the coffee plant. Those who knew about coffee did not want to share their good fortune. They had discovered a berry that seemed to have invigorating properties similar to those of alcohol!

Coffee had first arrived in Arabia from Ethiopia or West Africa around 600AD. Coffee soon spread through the entire Middle East, and there they were fanatical about not letting the secret of its cultivation out so they restricted its circulation.

~ ETIQUETTE NOTE ~
Some say that after dinner or supper, it is medicinally beneficial, as well as a perfect luxury.

For many years coffee beans could only leave the country after they had been cooked or dried to prevent the use of the seed germ by others.

Coffee should be black as hell, strong as death and sweet as love.
Turkish Proverb

The secret's out ...

By 1500 the Turks had introduced coffee to Eastern Europe. Vienna and Paris soon took to drinking coffee and it spread to Britain.

There was no chance of keeping the secret once the Dutch intervened. The Dutch took the bean to Ceylon and to the East Indies and then presented the coffee-loving King Louis XIV with a coffee plant which was to start the production of coffee in Martinique. Eventually the coffee plant was introduced to Brazil where it was established over a quarter of the country.

Traditional brews of ales ...

Coffee had a low profile with the people of Europe, who were steeped in their traditional brews of ales. However, Pope Clement VIII smelt the aroma of coffee, he expressed his delight and gave coffee his blessing, which then set the seal of approval for the Christian countries.

'Coffee causes much excitement
in the brain...'
Brillat-Savarin 1755–1826

Coffee still highly priced but popular ...

Coffee was first brought to England by Daniel Edwards in 1652; his Greek servant Pasqua Rosee, well understood the art of roasting the berries and preparing beverages. A coffee house was soon opened in George Yard, Lombard Street in London. In this way, coffee, although still highly priced, soon became popular.

The Americans favoured coffee, shunning the
drinking of tea because of the enormous import
taxes being charged on it.

In 1773, at the Boston Tea Party, the locals
showed what they thought of Britain by dressing up
as red Indians and tipping the expensive cargo from
the British merchant ships into the Boston harbour.

They then drank coffee all the more as an
act of defiance!

**Those who are exposed to morning and
evening dews find great support
from a cup of coffee.**

T.I.P.

It is said that our custom of tipping
arose from the coffee house days when
patrons had to place money in a box
marked T.I.P. - in order
To Insure Promptness.

COFFEE HOUSES

In the early days of coffee drinking it was difficult for the average person to make the brew successfully and the whole process was cloaked in mystery.

There soon appeared a variety of coffee houses where ordinary people could go to buy a cup of ready-prepared coffee and a club atmosphere developed around the drinking places.

It seems that no matter where these coffee houses were established, they had at least one thing in common – women were barred!

**'When we drink coffee,
ideas march in like the army.'
Honore de Balzac 1799-1850**

*P*enny Universities ...

In 1650 a Lebanese called Jacob opened the first coffee house in Oxford at the Angel Inn – and by the end of the 17th century there were two thousand coffee houses in London and in the provinces.

People who paid 1d or 2d membership could enter these coffee shops no matter what beliefs they had, their rank or occupation. There they would meet other business people, artists and members of every kind of profession. In the early 18th century, there was little effective communication and news could be most easily obtained at the coffee house.

*B*usiness centres ...

From one of these houses, kept by Edward Lloyd in Lombard Street, sprang up the original famous Lloyds underwriting establishment.

*'Then to Lloyd's coffee house he never fails
to read the letters and attend the sales.'*
Mr. Frederick Martin

Besides Lloyds, the coffee houses were the birth places of the London Stock Exchange which was based in Jonathan's Coffee House in Change Alley, the Bankers Clearing House, the Royal Society, *The Spectator* newspaper and other businesses.

Classless societies ...

For the main, all were treated as equals who went into these coffee houses. Customers had to take potluck as to where they would be seated. It wasn't expected of an ordinary person to give up his seat for an aristocrat!

When you needed friendly company you could always rely on one of the coffee houses to provide it.

The Turk's Head Coffee House was the meeting place of Dr.Johnson, who compiled the first English dictionary.

Different coffee houses for different people

The great fire of London in 1666 forced the coffee houses to move to new sites, often away from the very centre of the city.

MEDICAL MEN
patronised Bastions in Cornhill.

BOOKSELLERS AND AUTHORS
went to The Chapter in Paternoster Row.
Copyrights were bought here.

LAWYERS AND BARRISTERS
favoured The George in the Strand.

ESTATE AGENTS
frequented The London in Ludgate Hill.
Here, properties were auctioned by candlelight.

TORIES
met and relaxed in Ozindas.

WRITERS AND POETS
had their meeting place at Wills in Covent Garden.

'Let no man grumble when his friends fall off,
As they will do like leaves at the first breeze;
When your affairs come round,
one way or t'other,
Go to the coffee-house, and take another.'
Byron – (Don Juan)

Coffee coinage ...

At the height of their popularity coffee houses made their own coins to encourage business. They were a kind of trade token and with these coins, preferential treatment could be offered for a customer's loyalty. This continues in the form of modern day loyalty cards!

~ ETIQUETTE NOTE ~
Coffee should always be drunk from a cup -
It is considered the utmost bad manners to
pour it into the saucer!

Men's clubs

Once the cost of drinking coffee dropped and most men could afford to use the coffee houses, they lost their allure for the intelligentsia. Alcohol started being served and those who had given in to alcohol at one end of the bar could merely approach the other end and sober up with some coffee! The coffee houses became rowdy and were no longer acceptable to those who merely wanted a meeting place.

Coffee as a cure for a hangover?
'There is nothing more effectual
than this reviving drink,
to restore the senses that have brutified
themselves by immoderate tippling
of heady liquors.'
1675

The literary club - a peaceful haven

The fall from grace of the coffee houses led to the establishment of the literary and subscription clubs.

These clubs offered a peaceful haven to the gentlemen who would no longer tolerate the declining conditions in the coffee houses. Here would be protection from the common herd!

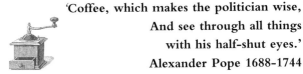

'Coffee, which makes the politician wise,
And see through all things
with his half-shut eyes.'
Alexander Pope 1688-1744

The Evils of Ale and The Virtues of Coffee
1674

'Coffee arrives, that grave and wholesome liquor
That heals the stomach, makes the genius quicker,
Relieves the memory, revives the sad
And cheers the spirits, without making mad.

It helps digestion, want of appetite,
And quickly sets consumptive bodies right.
Hush then, dull quacks, your mountebanking cease
Coffee's a speedier cure for each disease.

Own sobriety to be your drift,
And love at once good company and thrift,
To wine no more make wit and coyn a trophy
But come each night and frolique here in coffee.'

The Temperance Movement ...

Drunkenness was a great problem in the first half of the 19th century, and often the only place for any refreshment away from home was the public house.

Campaigners like John Wesley saw the need for non-alcoholic drinks to be served in places similar to the public houses.

Forerunners of modern coffee shops

The Coffee Palace of East London was opened in 1873, then came *The People's Cafes* in 1874. These were fashioned closely on the continental model introduced by Swiss-Italian adventurers in London. They were especially suited to the needs of clerks, shopkeepers and others engaged in business.

These cafes were the forerunners of our modern day coffee and tea shops.

> I have measured out my life
> with coffee spoons.
> T.S. Eliot 1888-1965

Ꙇyons Corner House ... *Intensely middle-class*

'I recall venturing one day into one of the Lyons (Corner House) restaurants just above Regent Street in Piccadilly and being struck with the size and importance of it even though it was intensely middle-class ... an enormous crowd of very commonplace people were there - clerks, minor officials, clergymen, small shop-keepers ... I recall being amused by the tall, thin, solemn English head-waiters in frock coats, leading the exceedingly bourgeois customers to their tables.'

T.Dreiser 'A Traveller At Forty.' (New York 1913)

Hitherto there had been nowhere respectable for mama and children to have a cup of coffee or midday meal. Prices, too, had been extortionate. These new coffee houses introduced to the Londoners, and later to the provinces, good cheap food with quite exceptional smartness and cleanliness.

~ ETIQUETTE NOTE ~
*Some eccentric people infuse coffee cold,
allowing it to stand for a long time,
and heating it just before serving, but this is
rather too elaborate a method to be
frequently adopted!*

FAMOUS COFFEE LOVERS ...

'Coffee is sweeter than honey,
better than a thousand kisses ...'
Sebastian Bach

'The drink that comforteth the brain
and heart and helpeth digestion.'
Bacon

'The morning cup of coffee has an exhilaration about it
which the cheering influence of the afternoon or evening
cup of tea cannot be expected to reproduce.'
Oliver Wendell Holmes Sr. 1891

'His most frequent ailment was the headache which he used
to relieve by inhaling the steam of coffee.'
Dr. Johnson on The Life of Pope

FAMOUS COFFEE LOVERS ...

*"Nothing'll make a father swear before the children
quicker than a cup of poor coffee.'*
K. Hubbard (Abe Martin on things in general)

*'Coffee falls into the stomach ... ideas begin to move,
things remembered arrive at full gallop ... the shafts of
wit start up like sharp-shooters, similies arise,
the paper is covered with ink ... '*
Honore de Balzac 1799 – 1850
(Who attributed his prolific writing career to
coffee drinking!)

**Beethoven meticulously counted out
60 beans for every cup of
coffee he consumed!**

~ ETIQUETTE NOTE ~
*Neat-handedness and judgement,
so necessary for cooking an omelette,
are quite as much required for
perfect making of coffee.*

Hints for The Best Coffee in the World
1887

*It requires merely care and common-sense to make
the best coffee in the world:-*

1. Those who have the means of roasting coffee beans
should always buy them unroasted.

2. The best way to roast coffee beans is in the frying pan!
The beans should be placed in the pan over a fire; stir
gently until they are a dark mahogany colour, take off the
fire and allow to cool.

3. They should be ground as soon as cool. Use a coffee
mill and do not let the grocer grind them for you
as you do not know how long they have been ground.

4. When the beans are roasted they should always be
kept in an air-tight receptacle, the best form being
wide-necked bottles with glass stoppers.

5. As soon as the coffee is ground, boiling water should
be poured upon it and it should be left near the fire for a
few minutes before pouring it out gently.

6. It can be strained through a fine filter or flannel bag
into the coffee pot for the breakfast table.

'No coffee can be good in the mouth
that does not first send a sweet offering
of odour to the nostrils.'
Henry Ward Beecher

HOW TO MAKE OTHER COFFEE DRINKS

Crème de Cacao

The best mocha coffee is roasted and ground until very fine. This is infused into brandy for ten days, then distilled in a double boiler. More coffee can be infused at this point if a stronger coffee is needed, then sugar is added and the liqueur is left overnight and filtered the following day.

Coffee Essence

Coffee essence is made as follows:- one part of coffee to three parts of water. Distil in the heat of 200 degrees fahrenheit in a closed vessel for 10 minutes, then strain and let it evaporate at a low temperature in a vacuum until reduced to one part.

HOW TO MAKE OTHER COFFEE DRINKS

Café à la Crème Frappé de Glacé

For a delicious breakfast during the summer heats, make a strong infusion of Mocha or Bourbon coffee; put it into a porcelain bowl, sugar it properly and add to it an equal portion of boiled milk, or one third of the quantity of rich cream. Surround the bowl with pounded ice.

This is excellent for those who had lost their appetite or who experienced general debility.

~ ETIQUETTE NOTE ~
*When a meal is ended, all men should stand
and the one nearest the door should open it
and hold it open until the ladies have all
passed through.
After that the men smoke and chat; coffee can
either be brought to them or they can go to
the drawing room for it.*

HOW TO MAKE OTHER COFFEE DRINKS

Coffee Royale

Gloria is a redolent mixture of coffee, loaf sugar and cognac.

To half a cupful of strong coffee add four large lumps of sugar; then pour over the back of your tea-spoon with a steady hand. Add an equal quantity of fine old cognac as you have of coffee; the spirit will, of course, float on the coffee, and great care must be taken that the two fluids mix not. Then light the brandy and, when the evil spirit has evaporated, stir the beverage and you will have one of the most delicious liqueurs imaginable; and independently of its exhilarating powers, it will be found to possess digestive qualities in no ordinary degree. This is strongly recommended to all dyspeptic people.

P.L. Simmads
'Coffee As It Is And As It Ought To Be.'

~ ETIQUETTE NOTE ~

*The butler and another servant take the coffee
to the ladies in the drawing room. The servant carries
a tray with coffee cups, milk and sugar -
and the butler follows him with a coffee pot
on a silver salver. Guests take cups into which
they put cream and sugar, then they put their
cups on the butler's salver, and he pours
coffee into them.*

After a heated argument between Winston
Churchill and Nancy Astor on some trivial
matter, Nancy shouted:

'If I were your wife I would put poison in your
coffee!'

Whereupon, Winston Churchill with equal
heat and sincerity answered:

'... and if I were your husband
I would drink it!'

(Nancy Astor was Countess Astor
1879 - 1964)

A French coffee maker that looked attractive on the breakfast table consisted of two glass globes, one above the other, with a spiral lamp beneath. The water is placed in the lower globe, and is forced up by the heat to the coffee, which is in the upper globe, from whence it is drawn off.

COFFEE RECIPES

Coffee Cake

1 teacup of sugar ½ teacup of butter
½ teacup treacle 1½ breakfast cups flour
1 teacup of cold, strong coffee
1 teaspoon each of salt, powdered cloves
and cinnamon

Thoroughly mix the salt, cloves and cinnamon with the flour. Cream the butter and sugar, add the treacle and beat well, then add alternately the flour and the coffee and 1 teaspoon bicarbonate of soda. Beat all thoroughly well together and bake about one hour in not too hot an oven.

COFFEE RECIPES

Coffee Bread

1lb flour	2oz butter
1½oz caster sugar	1 salt spoonful of salt
2 fresh eggs	Approx ½ pint milk
2 small teaspoonfuls baking powder	

Put three quarters of the flour into a basin, heat it until warm to the touch and add the salt and sugar. Put the butter and milk into a saucepan and stir until warm and well mixed. Make a well in the centre of the flour, add the warm milk and butter gradually and form into a smooth batter. Break in the eggs and beat well. Mix the baking powder with the remaining ¼lb of flour, and add this quickly to the batter the last thing. Half fill some greased patty pans, or small tins with this mixture and bake in a quick oven for 20 minutes.

Serve with fresh coffee.

COFFEE RECIPES

Coffee Fritters

Cut three milk rolls into even-sized pieces, about ¼ inch thick, and remove the crust. Put the slices in a pie dish, and over them pour about ½ pint of strong, clear coffee, flavoured with a few drops of vanilla essence.

When the bread has absorbed the liquid, but before it has become pulpy, dip the pieces into a thick pancake batter, so as to cover them completely.

Fry them golden brown in hot fat. Drain and dredge well with sugar and a little ground cinnamon. These are excellent served with stewed apples and custard.

COFFEE RECIPES

Coffee Pudding

5oz fine bread crumbs	2oz of candied peel
½ pint coffee	3oz sultanas
3oz sugar	2 eggs
Grated rind of 1 lemon	¼ pint milk

Put the bread into a basin, with the shredded peel, the grated lemon rind, the sultanas and sugar. Whisk the eggs and to them add the milk and the coffee, stir these into the dry ingredients. When well mixed, let all stand for 10 minutes, then pour into a greased mould and bake in a moderate oven.

COFFEE RECIPES

Coffee Junket

Put one pint of new milk into an enamelled saucepan, flavour it with 4 teaspoonfuls of very strong coffee, and add sugar to taste. Heat gently over the fire until at blood-heat, then pour it into a glass dish. Add immediately one tablespoonful of essence of rennet and stir two or three times.

Then put the dish into a cool place and leave it undisturbed for an hour. When set put whipped cream in little heaps on top.

~ ETIQUETTE NOTE ~
*Neat and tidy servants are essential to the credit
of a household; dirty and slovenly attendants
at table stamp it with vulgarity.
The black battle-stain on a soldier's face
is not vulgar,
but the dirty face of a housemaid is!*

FAMOUS COFFEE LOVERS ...

Voltaire was a habitual coffee drinker.

'A fig for partridges and quails,
ye dainties I know nothing of ye;
But on the highest mount in Wales
Would choose in peace to drink my coffee.'
Jonathan Swift 1667–1745.

Goethe, a much quoted German poet and writer, is
said to have been in a state bordering on
delirium because of drinking too much strong
coffee, the whole time he was writing
The Sorrows Of Werter!

FAMOUS COFFEE LOVERS ...

Napoleon abstained from the use of wines, but
drank coffee at all hours of the day, to revive the
spirits and invigorate the body.

Complacencies of the peignoir, and late
Coffee and oranges in a sunny chair.
Wallace Stevens 1879 - 1955. American Poet

'He was my cream, and I was his coffee -
And when you poured us together, it was something!'
Josephine Baker 1906–1975
(describing a royal affair!)

WISDOM IN THE COFFEE CUP

Any person in search of wisdom would come to consult one of the 'Cup Women' with a small bag of roasted beans.

One or more cups of aromatic drink would be prepared, and it was the custom to give the soothsayer a cup or two as well.

The spirit of the fortune teller's art certainly seems to have instilled itself in these women, for their popularity was enormous.

The first such fortune tellers to be recorded plied their trade in Paris at the beginning of the 18th century - then in Germany. They interpreted the coffee grounds and devoted themselves to the fate of their clients.

Now examine the grounds for the following symbols:-

WISDOM IN THE COFFEE CUP

Anchor   Hope and constant love

A cross   Anticipate a gentle, long life

Circle   Children

(A perfect and complete circle - a boy
An imperfect circle - a girl)

If alongside the circle, a crooked, wavy line is present, this signifies that the child will be blessed with great intelligence.

If the second line forms another circle, the child will be a genius.

Cross *(many)*   Expect a tumult of passion!

Flowers   Success

Line *(long)*   You will undertake a long
                      journey

Several lines   A happy old age

Serpent   Beware falsehood

Stars   Good and happy children

IN BRAZIL

At the turn of the last century there was a custom in Brazil concerning the giving of coffee beans.

When a child is born, a sack of the best beans is set aside as part of his inheritance. This sack, nearly always the gift of a close friend or relative, is guarded as a sacred thing. Nothing would induce a Brazilian to use coffee which had been given to a child. The precious sack is sealed and bears a card with all particulars concerning the kind of grain, its age, the date it was sealed and other details of the child's birth.

Usually the sack is opened when the child is grown and marries. Some of the stored coffee is used for the wedding feast, then the sack is again closed. It is then sent to the new home of the young couple and the contents should keep them in coffee for at least a year, thus the sack of coffee serves a double purpose: it is both a birth gift and a wedding present!

TURKISH COFFEE

Turkish coffee used to be made over a fire – and the recipe has not changed for centuries.

Coffee from Mocha was used for Turkish coffee. The ritual of serving the oldest and most respected guest first still exists in Turkey.

The grounds are pulverised and the coffee should be made in an 'Ibrik' which is a traditional long–handled copper pan. After the coffee has been brought to the boil three times using the equivalent amounts of coffee and sugar and only a small amount of water, it is left to stand for a few minutes to let the grounds settle.

The coffee is served in small cups which are never filled to the brim. *Filled cups are a sign of disrespect.*

COFFEE STALLS

In the middle of the 19th century coffee stalls were very popular. The owners would position themselves in the busiest parts of London. In 1865 there were more than three hundred coffee stalls in London and the average earnings of their proprietors was £1 a week. The approaches to the city were well occupied and at the foot of the bridges the stall-keeper would hail with fragrant aroma the passing workers. At the corner of wide, cold and desolate streets, his glowing charcoal would cheer the chilled and weary pedestrian; the clatter of his crockery must have been music to the ear and his cheery face in the candle-lamp a welcoming sight.

At that time, some 660,000 gallons of coffee were said to be sold each year on the streets of London - better a thousand times than a 'penneth o'gin' to keep out the cold. Half a mug of coffee, ½d; slice of bread and butter, ½d - the late worker could go home refreshed, the early worker could go on to work strengthened!

COFFEE CHAT ...

'The last proof that tea or coffee are favourable to intellectual expression is that all nations use one or the other as aids to conversation.'

Philip G. Hamerton - The Intellectual Life.

In Hawaii between 1810 – 1825 coffee was used as money (or at least a substitute for taxes).

In Brazil when they were trying to keep the price of coffee up they used coffee from bountiful harvests to stoke their locomotive engines!

At the start of the newly-formed state postal service it was a common practice to use coffee houses as receiving and distribution centres for overseas mail.

COFFEE CHAT ...

When coffee grew wild in north-east Africa the wandering tribesmen used it as a food. They would pound and grind the beans between stones, add some grease and use it to sustain them in their travels.

Benjamin Moseley M.D., Physician to the Chelsea Hospital, said in 1792:
'To constitutionally weak stomachs it affords a pleasing sensation; it accelerates the process of digestion, corrects crudities, and removes the colic and flatulence.'

Coffee is now grown in a band between 25 degrees north - and 30 degrees south of the equator where there is no frost, plenty of rain and a temperature between 18-24 degrees centigrade. It is successfully grown between the tropics of Cancer and Capricorn.

COFFEE TODAY

Coffee lovers in the past struggled to produce a good steaming pot of coffee, first teaching servants, then trying various services offered, such as 'London's first hot-drink vending machine' of 1895. This used the waste heat from gas street lamps to provide hot water! Since then many mechanical devices have been offered aiming to create the perfect cup of coffee.

1950s coffee bars

In the 1950s, coffee bars accompanied the new 'rock and roll' culture. The juke box and the coffee bar were made for one another - and coffee drinking has never looked back!

New variations

Now the aroma of freshly roasted coffee beans, with its promise of a perfect pot of coffee is familiar to coffee lovers today world-wide. Espresso, cappuccino and other delicious variations have stemmed from our changing lifestyle.

Espresso

Espresso coffee is the distinctive dark, strong coffee favoured in Italy. It is made by forcing steam through the finely ground, dark roasted beans. Espresso is drunk in smaller quantities and is slightly bitter and thick. Before the second world war the Italians were injecting steam through the coffee to make espresso, and shortly after they were invented, the espresso machines revived the custom of coffee drinking in this country through the new, modern coffee bars.

Latte

Steamed milk is added to espresso coffee to make this popular milky coffee.

'It diffuses a genial warmth that cherishes the animal spirits and takes away the listfulness and languor.'

Cappuccino

This hot, frothy, milky coffee is espresso with extras and was one of Italy's favourite drinks which spread throughout Europe in the 1950s. The name originated because the soft brown colour resembled the robes of the Capuchin order of monks.

Cappuccino soon became a world-wide favourite with the addition of whipped cream, cinnamon, cocoa powder or flaked chocolate!

'Coffee has stimulating, non-intoxicating and satisfying properties and is therapeutic. It speeds up the thought processes, the capacity for deduction and association is enhanced. Reactions are sharpened.'

A cup of coffee - real coffee, home-browned, home-ground, home-made, that comes to a golden bronze as you temper it with cream.

THE ETIQUETTE COLLECTION *Collect the set!*

ETIQUETTE FOR THE BRIDE
Traditional advice from times gone by to delight
and inspire today's bride.

ETIQUETTE FOR CHOCOLATE LOVERS
Temptation through the years.
A special treat for all Chocolate Lovers.

THE ETIQUETTE OF NAMING THE BABY
'A good name keeps its lustre in the dark.'
Old English Proverb

THE ETIQUETTE OF AN ENGLISH TEA
How to serve a perfect English afternoon tea;
traditions, superstitions, recipes and how to read your
fortune in the tea-leaves afterwards.

THE ETIQUETTE OF ENGLISH PUDDINGS
Traditional recipes for good old-fashioned
puddings – together with etiquette notes
for serving.

ETIQUETTE FOR GENTLEMEN
*'If you have occasion to use your handkerchief
do so as noiselessly as possible.'*

A Copper Beech Book makes the perfect gift.

Etiquette for the Traveller
'There is nothing that a man can less afford to leave at home than his conscience or his good habits.'

Etiquette for the Well-dressed Man
A man is judged by his appearance.
'If you wear a morning coat your trousers will show more and must therefore be absolutely blameless.'

The Etiquette of Motoring
'Never take a sharp corner at full speed. A walking pace would be much better.'

The Etiquette of Dress
Learn how to be correctly dressed for all occasions.
A fine gift for anyone with an interest in fashion.

For your free catalogue, write to:

Copper Beech Publishing Ltd
P O Box 159 East Grinstead Sussex England RH19 4FS

www.copperbeechpublishing.co.uk